Born To Rule:
Awaken the BornCEO Within You

7 Steps to Claiming Your Freedom & Living Your Purpose

Copyright © 2019 Coach Fard Bell & BornCEO, Inc. All rights reserved. No part of this book can be reproduced in any form without the written permission of the author and its publisher.

Table of Contents

Acknowledgements	4
Introduction: You Were Born To Rule!	6
My BornCEO Story	11
Chapter One: "B" is for Become...	13
Chapter Two: "O" is for Own...	22
Chapter Three: "R" is for Rule...	29
Chapter Four: "N" is for Never...	42
Chapter Five: "C" is for Clarify...	48
Chapter Six: "E" is for Execute...	65
Chapter Seven: "O" is for Overcome...	69
Other BornCEO Stories	73
Conclusion	99
Declarations	100
"BECOME WHO YOU WERE BORN TO BE"	101
Additional Resources	102

This book is dedicated to my beloved son Jacob Victorious Bell and to the next generation of world changers.

Your lives are God's gifts to this world!

Acknowledgements

To my Heavenly Father and the King of my crown... For being there when I felt alone, for showing me my purpose, and for trusting me with this assignment.

To my Dad... For proving that we can change our lives and for teaching me "if you want to change your life change the people you're around, change the places you go, and change the things you do."

To my Stepdad... For never making me feel like a stepson, for teaching me self-education, for warning me "If you don't learn how to work smart for yourself and your family, you'll spend the rest of your life working hard for someone else and their family".

To my Mom... For enduring the unthinkable to give us a better life, for reminding us to never give up on our dreams, and for demonstrating that education + inspiration + implementation = compensation.

To my big sister Angela... For standing up for me as a kid, for always believing in me, and for supporting me in all of my endeavors.

To Hannah... For being for being my best friend in this journey called life, for your transparent spirit, for reminding me who I am, and for being the greatest mother on the planet to our amazing son.

To my entire family... For all of your support, for your prayers, and for inspiring me to become who I am today.

To my friends… For helping me see my blind spots, for being a shoulder to cry on, and for making the journey so much fun.

To my mentors... For becoming so valuable, for paving the way, and for taking the time to lift up the next generation.

To my team for adding value to my life, for lending me your gifts, and for freeing me to do what I was born to do by doing what you were born to do. Malyssa… You Rock!

To my students, my clients, and to you… For allowing me to serve you, discovering who you are, becoming who you were born to be, and for doing what you were born to do to make this world a better place.

Introduction

You Were Born To Rule!

Before you were born, there was an invisible crown customized, crafted, and engraved specifically for you. The moment you arrived, your crown was taken and hidden from you; causing you to forget that you were born of royalty. You came from an invisible Kingdom where there is no such thing as poverty, sickness, lack, or limitations, but you came into a world filled with these foreign ideas. You were sent here on a special assignment to discover and use your unique power and gifts to help change the physical world to reflect the invisible world you come from. When you find your crown and put it back on, it will guide you to the domain you were born to rule. This domain belongs to you. It is the place where your gifts come alive, your influence becomes unstoppable, and you receive unlimited access to all of the resources you need, to do what you were born to do. Your purpose in life is to find your crown, put it back on, and rule your domain. You. Were. Born. To. Rule.

Imagine if you had unlimited access to money, resources, and good people to support you. All of your bills are paid, you are independently wealthy, and you no longer need to work for money. What would you do with your time? If you could only do one thing for the rest of your life to make a positive impact in this world, what do you think it would be?

What if you were born to be more than just another worker, just another taxpayer, or just another bill payer? What if you broke the chains and claimed your freedom? What if you put your crown back on and started ruling your own domain? What would happen if you started living like the leader you were truly born to be and inspired others to do the same? What would the world look like?

If you have ever felt stuck or overwhelmed by fear and circumstances, or have been bombarded with bills to pay, having little to no time to focus on your true purpose, it's not your fault. If there was a school that offered classes called "how to become independently wealthy and start living your true purpose", most of us would have signed up. Unfortunately, many of us didn't have that option.

I refused to let that stop me and I went on a search to find the answers I was looking for and to find the right mentors who could help me.

So I prayed and listened for guidance. Since the age of 14 I was inspired to read and listen to hundreds of books and audiobooks, watch hundreds of videos, and attend hundreds of seminars. I joined coaching programs and mastermind groups. I discovered a secret of the successful and started investing in my own transformation and self-education. Since 1986, I've invested hundreds of thousands of dollars and learned from hundreds of independently wealthy business leaders, millionaires, philanthropists, and humanitarians. I found great mentors and coaches with different areas of expertise and unique gifts. I met with greats like Dr. Myles Munroe, Jim Rohn, Harland Stonecipher, Dr. E.R. Braithwaite, Brian Tracy, Frank & Theresa AuCoin, John & Elizabeth Garner, Larry Smith, Les Brown, Robert Kiyosaki, Lisa Nichols, Darnell Self, Susie Carder, Brian Carruthers, John Addison, Brendon Burchard, Jeff Olson, Kevin Mack, Wynton Marsalis, Eric Worre, John C. Maxwell, Keith Battle, and many others. I got to meet and spend time with over a half dozen billionaires to learn how they think. Billionaires like Paul J. Meyer, Peter J. Daniels, Donald Trump, Sir Richard Branson, Bill Austin, and Tony Robbins. I was blessed to meet with both Paul J. Meyer and

Bill Austin and their families in each of their own homes.

By applying the principles I discovered along the way, I was not only able to discover what I was born to do, but also became financially independent and was able to retire 40 years early at the age of 22. That didn't mean I was rich with money, it meant I was rich with time. I had discovered the key to time freedom and had created a full-time retirement income long before reaching what others call "retirement age".

My mission in life is to inspire and equip the next generation of world changers to become financially independent and enjoy their lives while doing what they were born to do. I absorb everything I learn and use my gifts to inspire and teach others in a way that both teenagers and adults can understand. My dream is to bring all of those ideas, strategies, and personal experiences together in one place for those who don't want to wait 20 years and invest hundreds of thousands of dollars to discover what I've learned. So I finally created an online school at BornCEO.com Where we provide online courses, life and business coaching programs, and other resources to inspire and equip our students and clients become financially independent and do what they were born to do.

When you begin to take charge of your own life and start the process of becoming the leader you were truly born to be, we call you the BornCEO of You, Incorporated. Welcome to the BornCEO Movement!

If you believe in the power of personal and professional development to take your life, career, or business to the next level... This is the book you've been searching for. It's time to awaken the BornCEO within you!

My BornCEO Story

Repeat after me: "I was Born to Rule."

Although I've been blessed to break some of the chains in my life, make some good business decisions, retired 40 years early, and discovered what I was born to do, I've also made many mistakes and I'm still a work in progress. I have my flaws, opportunities for growth, and blind spots just like everyone else. In fact, if you really knew my story, you might be amazed that I'm still alive to tell it…

By the age of six years old I didn't want to be alive… I was dealing with struggles I didn't know how to handle and I had already faced several near death experiences from asthma attacks. Like many others I was severely teased in school. I had a massive overbite, my ears were too big for my head, sometimes my allergies were so bad I had to wear goggles to school, I wore embarrassing clothes, we moved so many times that I was almost always the new kid, and to top it all off, my name was Fard. (As you can imagine, it was hard being Fard). I thought maybe dying would take the pain away and I wouldn't have any more problems.

Everything changed when I discovered the seven steps to claiming your freedom and living your purpose. These principles have the power to transform millions of people into the leaders they were born to be. These principles transformed me from being a timid little boy wanting to die, to finding the courage to lead and live out my true purpose.

In the following chapters you will find seven steps that have transformed every day people into financially independent leaders who are doing what they were born to do. Each of the seven steps are hidden within the acronym B.O.R.N. C.E.O. As you apply each step in your own life, you will not only awaken the BornCEO within you, but also awaken the BornCEO within others. Enjoy!

Chapter One

"B" is for Become...
Become the King or Queen of Your Domain

Repeat after me: "There's a domain I was born to rule."

What domain were you born to rule? What problem were you born to solve and what gift were you born to serve to the world? Your domain is your area of gifting, passion, and purpose which evolves into your area of expertise. Your purpose in life is to discover the domain you were created to rule and rule it in partnership with your creator. When you fulfill that purpose, you bring honor to your creator and your life becomes a significant gift to your generation.

Shortly after I was born I began to face problems. At three years old I specifically remember walking through the hallway of my school. Two of my teachers didn't see me there and I overheard them laughing and making fun of my name. It was one thing to experience that coming from the other kids, but hearing it from my authority figures somehow convinced me that the kids were right and there was something wrong with me. I burst into tears and ran to hide under a table and wouldn't come out until my older sister had to came to get me. I didn't understand why people didn't like me and I was beginning to not like myself.

Over time, the seeds of self-doubt that were planted started to grow into negative beliefs about myself. I began to take on the characteristics of a shy and timid person. I became a target for bullying and other forms of abuse. I hardly even opened up to talk to others until high school. I wanted to run away from my problems and escape the pain.

Have you ever tried to run away from a problem instead of facing it? Sometimes the problem seems to go away, and other times it keeps coming back or gets worse. There are certain problems we were born to solve. We were born to solve those problems, not run from them. The good news is that we are already gifted to solve the problems we were born to solve. There are some gifts we have that we may never discover until the right problem comes along to draw it out of us. In order to rule your domain you must become a master problem solver.

When problems come your way, let them remind you that you are in training to rule your domain. Problem solving is like weight lifting. Start by solving small life, career, and business problems and as you get stronger you can handle bigger problems. To put it in financial terms, people who solve thousand dollar problems earn thousands, and people who solve billion dollar problems earn billions. How much we earn is determined by the size of the problems we solve and the number of people we serve. That's why you never have to wait for someone else to give you a job or a pay raise. Just start solving bigger problems and serving more people. Eventually your refined gifts and skills can become so valuable that the people who need what you have want to hire you. There are some problems we can solve on our own and others that require more help. This is why it is important that you develop healthy win/win relationships with others who have the skills, gifts, and resources that you don't have. Your gift becomes a win for them and their gift become a win for you.

Before I understood this principle, I felt like the victim of my problems. I was like Pacman in one of my favorite video games running from away from the ghosts. When I finally realized that there were certain problems I was born to solve, it was as if I received my power and then the ghosts started running from me.

When I was six years old an angel literally appeared to me in a dream. I still remember it like it was yesterday. In the dream, I was playing with other kids on a huge playground surrounded by a beautiful blue background. The ball we were playing with rolled away from the scenery and I ran after the ball away from the other kids and the playground. As I approached the ball I could no longer hear the sound of the children playing. It was very quiet and peaceful. When I reached down to pick up the ball, I saw a tall translucent figure of light, at least ten times my height! I stood there in awe of its presence, and I was immediately filled with a love I don't have words to describe. I felt safe and the voice said "I am with you and I am pleased. You're going to be ok. I'm keeping you alive because there is something important you were born to do."

When I woke up, I could still feel the power of the angel's presence and I never wanted it to leave me. I wasn't religious, but I knew it was God and I wanted Him to stay proud of me. I left that dream knowing that He knew me, loved me, was proud of me, had big plans for me, and that He was protecting me.

The next day I was on my way home from playing at my friend's house. It was raining and as I ran across the road I slipped and fell in the middle of the street. My friend's house was on a hill and cars would come speeding over it. A huge truck came speeding over the hill and before I could get up I heard the tires screeching behind me. I couldn't get up fast enough. As I laid on the ground with my back facing the oncoming truck, listening to the screeching tires, I knew I was about to die. Suddenly and miraculously, the truck came to a halt and its front tires barely tapped my back. As I crawled out from under the bumper, I saw the driver looking for my body underneath the truck. When he saw me stand up he was shaking and crying in shock that I was alive. At that moment I remember what the Angel whispered in my dream: "I am with you and I am pleased. You're going to be ok. I'm keeping you alive because there is something important you were born to do."

That dream was followed by several near death experiences when I knew I should have died, but His presence was with me. As I mentioned I had really bad asthma as a child, and some of my asthma attacks should have taken me out, but I survived. Between the experience in my dream, and firsthand experiences of divine protection, I chose to believe that I was being prepared to fulfill a divine assignment. Most of us have had near death experiences whether we are aware of them or not. Some call them a coincidence. Some say coincidence is simply God's way of remaining anonymous. I believe as long as we are alive we have a purpose to fulfill. We just have to figure out what our purpose is.

Figuring out my purpose became like putting together a jigsaw puzzle without being able to see what the end result was supposed to look like. What do you do in a situation like that? You have to become a problem solver. Obviously running away from my problems wasn't going to solve anything. I had to face them head on.

I knew there was something I was born to do, I just needed to figure out what it was. I had a new reason to live and if I was going to be solving problems all my life I might as well find a way to enjoy it. I made a game out of discovering my purpose. I guess we can call it "putting together the pieces of our life purpose puzzle." (Try to say that five times fast.) I'm forever grateful to my mom for involving me in the performing arts growing up. It allowed me to visibly see the gifts and talents of others.

Throughout my life I could hear the voice from my dream whispering "Everyone has a gift and a purpose that I've given them, but many are disconnected from me. You're going to help people understand what I created them to do and help free them to do it." Although I had no clue what that meant at the time, it was a major piece to my life purpose puzzle that kept coming back to me over the years. It wasn't until I developed a burning desire to know what I was born to do, that I started (not passively), but actively seeking my purpose. The more I searched the more pieces I found. Along the way I met purpose driven mentors like the great Keith Battle, Dr. Myles Munroe, and many others who helped me understand how to put those pieces together.

Hopefully you're not sitting back passively waiting for an angel to show up to convince you that there is a problem you were born to solve. If you are however, allow me to be your angel today and receive this message that I've been sent to deliver to you right now… There's a problem in this world and YOU were born to solve it! Build your problem solving muscles by solving the problems that come your way as practice. If you don't know how to do something ask yourself "what can I read, listen to or watch until I figure it out?" If that doesn't work ask "who can I ask or recruit to help me solve this problem?" Be like an ant. No matter what obstacle you put in its way, an ant will explore every single option until it finds a way to accomplish what it set out to accomplish. That is the spirit of a problem solver.

Some of my favorite books and resources for discovering the domain you were born to rule include:

"Kingdom Citizenship" by Myles Munroe
"Purpose Driven Life" by Rick Warren
"Strength Finders 2.0" by Tom Rath
Personality types: CoachFardBell.com/type

If you need additional resources or support contact me at CoachFardBell.com/support

Chapter Two

"O" is for Own...
Own Your Choices

Repeat after me: "I am the BornCEO of my choices."

Who is responsible for how your life turns out? What has to change in order for you to take your life to the next level? What is your plan to become to step up as the BornCEO of your life?

Although arguably there may be a few exceptions, the life we each live today is mostly the result of all the choices we've made (or have not made) over the past five years. More importantly, the choices we make now will greatly impact how our lives turn out in five years. We have two choices. Choice #1 is to take responsibility for the choices we've made (to eat for pleasure or eat for health, to save and invest money or to spend money, to make emotional deposits into those we love or make emotional withdrawals, to study and practice or to just wing it, to only rely on our job or to work to secure our financial future or to work our financial freedom plan outside of our job, to develop better skills or to rely only on the skills we currently have, to invest in mentors and coaches or to do everything on our own, to give our very best or to just get by). The list of choices we make go on and on. Choice #1 says "If I'm satisfied or dissatisfied with any area of my life, career, or business and I stay that way, it's because of a choice or series of choices that I made. I can change my life by changing my choices. If I want things to change I can change. I am the BornCEO of my choices." Choice #2 says "It's not my fault I'm in my situation, it's because of circumstances outside of my control and there's nothing I can do to change". Even if there are circumstances outside of our control, there is always something we can do. We choose a new path or choose a new perspective. When we own our choices, we activate our power to change.

When I was a teenager my biological dad taught me a simple lesson about choices that I'll never forget. He told me he had made some choices he wasn't proud of that kept him away from me as a kid. I was raised by my mom and stepdad. When I asked how he was able to completely quit smoking, quit drinking, and turn his life completely around, he gave me his simple formula for change. He said, "Sonny, if you ever want to change something, change the people you're around, change the places you go, and change the things you do, but you have to really want to change."

Life is about choice management. The key is to decide what you want your life, career, business, or ministry to look like and allow your vision and goals to influence your choices. Your vision and goals should have veto power over your decisions. Everyone knows the proverb "where there is no vision, the people perish". In others words, without a healthy vision and healthy goals to guide us we make poor choices that lead to our downfall. Ask yourself "Is what I'm about to do going to take me closer to or further away from my goal?" It's important to acknowledge that the choices of our past have led us to the life we live now, and the daily choices we are making now and over the next few years are creating the life we will live a few years from now. Ask yourself, "what can I do every day or every week that will almost guarantee that I will achieve my goal?"

Listen to the audiobook "Challenge to Succeed" by Jim Rohn. For me it is still one of the most life changing audiobooks of all time. Two of my other favorite books on the power of choice are "The Slight Edge" by Jeff Olson, and "The Compound Effect" by Darren Hardy. Both authors were also mentored by Jim Rohn along with a multitude of other great speakers, mentors, and coaches.

One of the best days of my life was the afternoon I spent with the late, great, Jim Rohn. I can still hear his entertaining and expressive voice saying, "Success is easy." When he said that I couldn't help but wonder, if success is so easy, how come more people aren't more successful?

"What's easy to do is just as easy not to do." He explained. It's easy to eat an apple a day. The problem is, it's just as easy to eat a candy bar a day! In other words, don't make success harder than it really is. You don't always have to do complicated things in order to be more successful. If you take any area of your life and start doing the simple things that you can do every day, then over time you will become more successful in that area automatically. As the old saying goes "you will reap what you sow." The key to success is to practice simple daily disciplines that make you successful over time. On the contrary, the key to failure, is practice simple daily errors in judgment that make you unsuccessful over time. This applies to any area of your life that you want to improve. Mr. Rohn reminds us of the old saying, "An apple a day, keeps the doctor away." What if that's true? If one person eats an apple a day, and another person eats a candy bar a day, by the end of the week there's no apparent difference between the two people. By the end of the month, there might still be no apparent difference. But repeat that process over the next five years and the results will catch up to them. The impact of our choices don't usually show up right away, but they always show up over time.

If everyone who ate one donut instantly gained 50 lbs., most people would never eat a donut. If everyone who smoked one cigarette or drank one sip of alcohol died instantly most people would never smoke or drink. If everyone had a beautiful beach body after their first time exercising or everyone got rich the first time they invested 10% of their income, more people would consistently exercise and invest at least 10% of their income. The reality is, people do gain 50 lbs. eating donuts, die from smoking or drinking, become physically fit from exercising, and become wealthier from investing, but it's not instant. It doesn't happen overnight. Results take time. I don't like the saying "everything in moderation". It makes me cringe every time I hear it. Yes, some things are ok in moderation, but when we live according to our vision and goals we realize that some things should just be left alone altogether and other things are worth turning into lifestyle habits. Habits put results on autopilot.

The 5% who understand and practice these principles succeed in achieving their goals, and the 95% who neglect these principles don't. The key is to invest more time around the 5% to pick up their good habits and invest less time around the 95% to avoid their bad habits. There's an old saying "If you want to be successful, look at where the majority are going and go the opposite direction." Apparently there's some wisdom in that statement. It's easy to take a walk for 30 minutes a day, but it's easier not to. It's easy to save a dollar a day, but it's easier not to. It's easy to read 10 pages a day or listen to 30 minutes of a book or audiobook to grow spiritually, mentally, or professionally, but it's easier to watch the news, a TV show or listen to the radio. It's easy to carve out 30 minutes a day to study or practice, but it's easier to go hang out. Even by not choosing we make a choice. My next door neighbor taught me that it always takes work to maintain a weedless garden, but it takes no effort to grow weeds. By choosing not to pull the weeds, we automatically choose to let them grow.

3 keys to making better choices

1. Get inspired! Become vision and goal directed.
2. Get a good plan. Ask yourself the ownership question: "What can I do every day or every week that will almost guarantee that I achieve my goal?"
3. Get around people who are going or already are where you really want to end up. You really do become like the five people you spend the most time around. With that in mind, who are the people you need to spend less time around? Who are the people you need to spend more time around? One of the resources we provide to our students and clients is our weekly coaching mastermind. It's designed to help you clarify your goals, develop a winning plan, and execute your plans on a consistent basis. To learn more create your free account at BornCEO.com and follow the 3 steps inside of the Welcome Center.

Chapter Three
"R" is for Rule...
Rule Your Time

Repeat after me: "I am the BornCEO of my time."

Where will you find the time to do what you were born to do? How can you free more of your time? What is your freedom plan? Whatever you trade the rest of your time for is what you've traded the rest of your life for. What are you willing to trade the rest of your life for? This life is measured in time.

Sometime around the age of 14, I had moved in with my stepdad and my younger brother. I needed male guidance and I was auditioning for an amazing performing arts high school called Duke Ellington School of the Arts in Washington, DC. My dad loved learning and spent reading and listening to audiobooks. At, I was listening to The Science of Personal Achievement by Napoleon Hill. I learned that successful people budget their time the same way successful people budget their money. It was the first time I understood the value of time.

I realized that we're only given 24 hours in a day. If we use 8 of them for rest, that leaves us 16 hours each for everything else that's important to us. I took Napoleon Hill's advice and wrote out a time budget for the first time ever. I wrote down what a day in my dream life looked like. I wrote out exactly what to do with the 16 hours I had left in the day. I was beginning a practice I later learned is the secret of many multi-billionaires. One of the differences between those who struggle to earn a good living and those who earn billions in the same calendar year, is that the most successful people I've met schedule everything in the order of their most important and highest payoff priorities. When I finished my first time budget, I was inspired and impressed! That was until I realized I left something out. I forgot to include time for a job. I went from inspired to depressed! All of my dreams came crashing down in one single moment. Even at 14 I wished there was a way to enjoy my life and live my purpose without having to worry about how the bills would get paid.

One night I was watching a late night infomercial. Most of them were about how to build wealth. Once I saw passed the get rich quick hype I learned a major principle that would become the best time management secret I've ever discovered. I found out retirement has nothing to do with age once you learn how create early retirement income. Those who accomplish this do so by creating, building, or buying income producing assets which allow them to retire early. This is the essence of working smarter instead of harder so we can claim our freedom while enjoying our lives and living our purpose. This new discovery definitely captured my imagination and held my attention! That was when I learned that the key to time freedom is to create, build, or acquire income producing assets that generate "passive" or "residual" income. One of the infomercials I saw was selling a course that got me excited about creating rental income and I asked my dad if we could get the course so I could get a head start before I turned 18. He told me he already had it, and said, "What do you think your mom has been doing all this time?" I found out my mom had studied and most importantly practiced those same principles and started acquiring rental properties at the age of 19! That was my introduction to the concepts of "leverage", "time freedom", and what I call "early retirement income" which led me to financial independence from my jobs. I started seeking passive residual income opportunities the way most people seek a good paying job. My first major goal was to retire before age 25 to do what I was born to do, but I had to learn find the right mentors and develop the right plan.

Over the years, I have invested time and money reading some of my favorite books like "Multiple Streams of Income" by Robert Allen, "Rich Dad, Poor Dad" & "Business of the 21st Century", both by Robert Kiyosaki, "The Millionaire Messenger" by Brendon Burchard, and "Dot Com Secrets" by Russell Brunson.

What's your plan to make a living while doing what you love? There are three major options I recommend. While any of the following plans are viable, I recommend that every BornCEO does something to create passive income so your income doesn't stop when you are busy enjoying your life, spending time with your family, and doing what you were born to do. Passive income also allows you to do what you love whether you get paid for it or not. This way, you don't burn out or lose your passion because you end up having to do it for the money. Here are the three of the options I recommend.

Option 1. Monetize Your Passion:

Many people choose this option because they want to get paid to do what they love without working to create another stream of income at the same time. In some cases it may not be ideal to earn passive income from your passion, in which case I would recommend combining options 1 and 2.

My passion is coaching and mentoring. That's what I was born to do. When you get good at your gift, people who need your gift become willing to pay you for it. Over the years, people told me I was really good at listening to their problems and helping them get unstuck. One of my friends called me a life coach in high school. Eventually people started asking to hire me to coach them through their life issues.

When I started succeeding in business, I got good at helping people get unstuck in their business. So, eventually, people started asking to hire me to help them get unstuck in business. That's how BornCEO Academy was born. As a coach I studied how other successful authors, speakers, and coaches monetized their gifts and I invested the time, effort, and money to implement those strategies to help fund my life mission.

I grew up in the performing arts with many of my friends who are highly gifted musicians and artists. Some of us were good at what we did and others were clearly gifted to do what they did. One time I flew back home to Washington, DC and met up with friends from high school who were performing. I was amazed to see their gifts in action. I'm still amazed. When I spoke to one of my friends afterward, and complimented her on how amazing she was, she said, "Thanks but I don't enjoy anymore." "What do you mean?" I asked. "I used to play because I loved it, but now that I have a family support, I do it because I have to." Hearing that broke my heart and is the reason I recommend starting option #2 as early as possible in life.

Option 2. Build Passive Income Outside of Your Purpose

Building passive income outside of your purpose allows you to do what you love whether you get paid for it or not. I started with Option 2 for a couple of reasons.

A. I knew the older I got the more expenses I would have to take on and I wanted to grow my passive income before I started taking on too many expenses.

B. I was still figuring out what my purpose was, so I couldn't monetize it anyway.

Because I started with Option 2, I was able to create a full time retirement income by the age of 22 and retire from corporate America 40 years early. My passive income allows me to pursue my passion whether I get paid for it or not. When I do get paid for it, the income from my passion allows me to reinvest in my dreams and serve more people.

Since then, I've earned passive residual income from several sources including:

Rental income

Products

Book royalties

Interest from loans

Affiliate Marketing

Membership subscriptions

Network Marketing

Before any of my passive residual income sources became significant "streams" of income, they started off as little drizzles of income. In order for a drizzle to become a significant stream of income, you have to put in the work to implement the right marketing and sales strategies. I call them "product pipelines". A product pipeline delivers two things. It delivers your product or service to the people who are willing to give you money for it, and it delivers the money they give you into your bank account or pockets. Some people try to build too many streams at the same time and instead of building a solid stream of passive residual income, they end up multiple drizzles of income. Drizzles of income are not large enough or consistent enough to replace a full-time income. It requires significant work, focus, and consistency to create a full time stream of passive residual income no matter what you do, but when your product pipeline is finally built and all of the leaks are plugged, it like you're growing your own money tree that can provide sustainable passive residual income for your family for generations to come.

My first full time stream of passive income came from my network marketing business. For the reasons above, I only have one network marketing business in my passive income portfolio. When you find the right one and built it properly, there's no reason to look for another one. Even though I was a full-time student working full time jobs, I was taught by the masters how to create a full-time income even though I only had 10 hours a week to grow my business. I simply put a full time effort into those 10 hours a week.

Option 3. Build Passive Income Outside Your Passion while Monetizing Your Passion

This is a combination of options 1 and 2. You can also create, build, or acquire income producing assets while earning income doing what you love. Some of my students and clients invest in rental properties, some are building a network marketing business, some create and market digital products, some save and lend their money to others in exchange for interest, and I help others some systemize their existing business so someone else can run it without them having to be their. There are plenty of ways to design your own customized freedom plan while doing what you were born to do. If you need support create your free account at BornCEO.com and follow the 3 steps inside of the welcome center.

Because I executed the plan that my success coaches helped me put together, I now have a full time retirement income from Option 2 which allowed me to retire from corporate America 40 years early and now I also earn a full time income from my passion. The process isn't as difficult as it sounds. Use those 3 options to help you determine what the best route is for you.

Rank the following options 1-3 in order of your inclination to use that specific plan.

Option	
Option One: Monetize Your Passion	
Option Two: Build Passive Income OUTSIDE of Your Passion	
Option Three Passive Income Outside Of Passion & Monetize Your Passion	

Last time I checked Corporate America and the government had a passive residual income plan called retire at 62. I think most of us prefer my plan better. I've met many people who went for corporate America's plan because that's what they were taught to do. They worked for 30-40 years, only to find out that their retirement income is not enough or the retirement program no longer exists by the time they hit retirement age. If you rely on government or corporate America to handle your retirement, be aware of the risks. You may be playing Russian roulette with your financial future. Real financial security comes from developing multiple streams of passive income and from developing the skills to create income with or without your job. Building passive income is a major key to ruling your time.

I won't go into much detail in this chapter, but whenever I help a client evaluate their freedom plan, I think of the 10 components of a product pipeline. Whenever a business is struggling it simply means there's a leak in one or more areas of the pipeline. In one of the following chapters I will lead you through the basic steps for designing and plugging the leaks in your product pipelines.

If you choose to start a company from scratch, you and your team are solely responsible for plugging all 10 leaks. If you buy a franchise many of the systems are provided for you in exchange for a significant investment and you're usually responsible for all of your expenses like renting a location and hiring your staff, etc. If you join a network marketing business, the company you join usually has a corporate staff in place and "upline" success coaches that either plug most of the leaks for you or teach you their system for plugging the leaks. The investment is often around $500 or less.

For people who want to start a business, but don't have a lot of time, money, or experience, joining a good network marketing company and plugging into a team that has a good system is the best place to start.

Chapter Four

"N" is for Never…
Never Stop Growing

Repeat after me: "I am the BornCEO of my mind."

It's time to grow! What areas of your life need grow in order serve you gift to the world? What is your customized personal growth plan? Start investing in yourself this month.

The best investment you can ever make is in the discovery and development of your own true identity, gifts, passion, and purpose, and in the development of the right mindset, skills, systems, people, and resources you need to deliver your gifts to world. If you knew you that investing in yourself would provide you with an infinite return on your investment, how much time, energy, and money would you willing to invest each month in your own personal, business, and leadership development?

How much money time, energy, and money do we spend on things that neither grow our impact nor our income? When you invest in your own personal, business, and leadership development, you increase your value both in society and in the marketplace. This type of development is a transformation process. When you develop the courage to let go of your old mindset and make this transformation, a whole new world of abundance is revealed to you that seems to be hidden from others in plain sight. opportunities will present themselves to you that you were not ready to receive before. You will have access to ideas, resources, and people that you didn't seem to have access to before.

Personal development is the process of transforming into the best version of your true self. Think of personal development like developing your total self. When I think of my total self I remind myself that I am a spirit, with a soul, inside of a body. I am not my physical body. I am a spirit with a soul (mind, emotions, and will). My physical body carries me (spirit) and my soul (my mind, emotions, and will) in order to fully function in a physical world. Personal development includes nurturing our true self (spirit), developing our mind, emotions, and will (soul), and taking care of our physical health (body).

Most people simply conform to the world around them. They believe what most people believe, they think how most people think, they feel how most people feel, they do what most people do, and they live like most people live. We were not born to conform to the world around us. We were born to transform the world around us. In order to transform the world, we must first be transformed into who we were born to be. We must renew our minds. We must change how we think.

When I think of transformation I often think of a caterpillar. When a caterpillar is ready to transform, it separates from its old environment by creating a cocoon around itself. The cocoon contains everything the caterpillar needs to transform into a butterfly. It simply needs to stay inside of its cocoon long enough to make the transformation. I was 14 when I started customizing my own personal growth plan. I started looking for new professors (aka mentors and coaches) outside of formal education. I needed mentors and coaches to help me discover and develop my true identity, my primary gift, the right mindset, the right skills, and a plan to free my time to do what I was born to do. Like a caterpillar I didn't have the wings to physically leave my environment yet. The community around me was still the same, including poverty, sickness, crime, drugs, and violence. It was the community within me that began to change. The coaches and mentors who produced the books, audiobooks, and videos, and courses became my new community. I brought "home" better values, ideas, beliefs, and strategies into my cocoon.

As a high school musician, some of my musician friends didn't understand why I was listening to audiobooks instead of music half the time. In college some people would come into my dorm room snack shop and laugh at the "motivational stuff" I was listening to. I tried to explain the difference between "motivational stuff" and educational stuff, but many were more interested in going to nightclubs like most people our age. Sometimes I wondered if I was missing out on my childhood, but I went to see for myself, I quickly realized I was more interested in becoming financially independent, traveling the world, and enjoying my life while living my purpose. I guess I have a different idea of fun.

My personal development accelerated when I discovered seminars. I learn well in a classroom environment where I can see, listen, take notes, interact with other classmates, and sense things intuitively. I did well in high school and usually enjoyed it. I just wanted to learn things that weren't being taught in school like how to discover my gifts and passion, how to manage money, how to become financially independent, and how to think like an entrepreneur. Those topics are about self-education and financial education usually found outside of formal education. All 3 forms of education are important, but most people only receive formal education in school. I found self-education and financial education in books, audiobooks, videos, seminars, networking opportunities, and conventions. Educational seminars, conventions, and mastermind retreats became my classrooms outside of school.

One day I was investing an afternoon with John C. Maxwell and received one of the best pieces of advice I've ever heard about self-development. He said, "Invest the majority of your time and resources working in your strength zone". On a 1 to 10 growth scale, it's almost like our God given talents, gifts, and abilities start off as a 7 or 8. Our job is to discover them and develop them into a 9 or 10. The problem is you can invest time, money, and energy for the rest of your life and only improve 1-2 notches on a 1-10 scale. If you focus all of your time and effort on your weaker abilities (where you only score a 1 or 2), the best you'll become is a 3 or a 4. There's a reason people don't hire 3's or 4's. In fact you get fired for performing at a level 3 or 4. People always hire 9's or 10's and pay good money to see them in action. You will make the greatest impact in the world when you become a 9 or 10. John Maxwell's advice was "If you want to become a 9 or 10, invest the majority of your time, energy and resources where you're already a 7 or an 8. When you improve 1 or 2 notches you'll become a 9 or 10".

It's often said "if your [reason] 'why' is strong enough you will figure out the 'how'". I agree with at statement to some degree, but I've seen many people who have very strong reasons "why", but they still feel stuck. The reason I've discovered, is that you "Who" is more powerful than your "why". Your "who" is your true identity. Your true identity is the image you were given by your creator. In a car, your "why is like the gas pedal, and your "who" is like the brake. You can slam on the gas pedal as hard as you can, but if your foot is still on the brake, you're not going anywhere. You're just burning rubber. Other coaches, mentors, and trainers start with "why" and what to read or do. At BornCEO Coaching, we start with "who" you were born to be. When you discover your "who", your "why" can start working for you. When you discover the power of your "who", and put your crown back on, you activate the power to rule your domain.

Chapter Five
"C" is for Clarify...
Clarify Your Vision

Write the vision and make it plain on tablets, that he might run who reads it.
- Habakkuk 2:2

"What is your dream? What will be required in order for it to become a reality? And what is your plan to pull it off?" Those are some of the questions I ask in my online "Best Year Ever" Workshop, available inside of the welcome center when you login at BornCEO.com.

"Imagine if you had unlimited access to money, resources, and good people to support you. All of your bills are paid, you are independently wealthy, and you no longer need to work for money." If you could only do one thing to make a positive impact in this world, what would it be?" Grab a pencil or pen and use the following space to write your answers.

One day I was attending a retreat where my friend and mentor John Gardner was speaking. He gave the best definition of a plan I'd ever heard when he said, "A plan is simply a written to-do list of everything needed to achieve your goal, prioritized, scheduled, and checked off." Henry Ford is quoted for saying "thinking is the hardest work there is", that's why so few people engage in it. My observation is that most people work hard and think they're smart. It's time to for us to start thinking hard and working smart.

Let's start right now. What will be required in order for your dream to become a reality? There are two types of people in this world. There are those who have a dream and are looking for right resources, and there are those who have the resources, but are looking for the right dream. Never put the "how?" before your "why?", and never put the "how?" before the power of your "who".

Start writing down why your dream is important in this world. What problems can your dream solve both directly and indirectly? Who are all of the people behind the causes, organizations, agencies, that will benefit from the success of your dream? Think about it and write down everything you can think of in the following space.

Where is your written plan to make it happen? Remember, there's a problem in this world and you were born to solve it. You are uniquely gifted to solve the problem you were born to solve. Develop a plan to serve your gift to the world. Think of your purpose is your area of expertise. Your area of gifting, passion and purpose will become your expertise and is the domain you were born to rule. Think of your gift like a product or service you provide. In order to reach the masses with your gift think like an entrepreneur.

Entrepreneurs put systems and teams together to create profitable products and services that solve problems for a specific group of people. They deliver those products or services through what I call "product pipelines". There are 10 basic components of a product pipeline. When combined, the ten components make up an acronym for "PRODUCT PIPELINES": (P. P. I. P. E. L. I. N. E.S.). Imagine you're going to start or grow a business, write down your answer to each question under the following 10 components. Use additional paper if needed.

1. Product/Service Creation.

What products or services might you offer?

2. Prospecting/Lead generation

What do the people who would buy it or fund it have in common and why would they buy or fund it? Where can you find them? Where are they already looking that you may want to place your advertisement? Are there enough of them to serve and sustain your vision?

3. Inviting/Advertising

What questions could you ask in your marketing about their desire, need, and/or problem that would grab their attention and make them realize they need and want to learn about what you offer? What outcome or result do they want so bad they would pay good money for it? What pain do they want to get rid of so bad they would pay good money for it?

4. Presenting your offer effectively

What are all of the reasons they would buy? What are all of the concerns they would have about buying? How could you respond in a way that removes their concerns and makes them almost beg you for your solution? What stories and examples can you share?

5. Enrolling/Closing Effectively

What closing questions could you ask your potential buyer (during and after your presentation) to lead them to a final decision to buy and finally get their problem solved? What can you do to follow up with those who are interested, but aren't ready today?

6. Leveraging/Systemizing/Staffing

What procedures, systems, and people could you put in place to handle business growth so the business can run smoothly without you being involved?

7. Insurance/Legal protection

What kind of licenses, insurance coverage, or legal services would you need to put in place to protect your business?

8. Net Profits/Cash Flow Management

What accountant and or bookkeeper can you talk to about planning and managing your income and expenses?

9. Evolving/Managing Changes

What events could take place in your industry, the economy, etc. that would cause you to change how you do business? How could you respond successfully?

10. Scaling/Expanding

What can you do to multiply your profits and expand what's already working?

This is just a basic introduction to the 10 components and provides a basic framework for evaluating your business or idea, plugging the leaks in your plan, and determining whether or not it's worth pursuing. Use these questions and your answers when consulting with your coaches and advisors. For support with this contact me at CoachFardBell.com/support.

Chapter Six

"E" is for Execute...
Execute Your Plans

All hard work brings a profit, but mere talk leads only to poverty. - Proverbs 14:23

It's implementation time! What do you need to implement first? What holds you back from executing your plan on a higher level? What is your implementation strategy to keep you moving forward?

At the age of 16, I attended a free seminar (because I could afford the price). At the seminar, they said, "Some of you want more." And I said, "Yep, that's me!" And they said, "You've got an overview of our system, but we've got a three day workshop to deep dive into the program and give you step by step instructions on how to create passive income from real estate."

At this point, my hand was in the air, I was excited, and ready to enroll in the program! Then they said it. "It's a $20,000 value, but we're giving it to you guys for only $2,000!" I went from excited to disappointed in a split second. I knew it was worth it, and I wanted to go so bad, but I was exactly

$2,000 short of $2,000. It didn't stop me because I knew that successful people don't say, "I can't afford it." They ask, "How CAN I afford it?" I needed a way to fund my financial education and I knew it was time to make a plan and execute it. I started asking the right question: "how can I make enough money to pay for my education?"

Remember that our mind is like an infinite search engine, but even more powerful than technology. The quality of the questions you ask will determine the results you get back. As I continued to ask the right questions a suppressed memory came back to me that gave me an idea for my plan. It was seven years earlier and I was in the 4th grade. While I was waiting at a bus stop I found a quarter on the ground and wanted to use it to buy candy with my friend at the convenient store right across the street from the bus stop. I never had money to buy candy before, so this was my first chance! I tried to convince one my friends to buy a pack of pixy stix and I would contribute my 25 cents in exchange for 3 straws. (It was like flavored sugar inside of a straw). My first plan didn't work because they didn't want to spend all of their candy money on pixy stix. I needed a new plan. I thought to myself "maybe three of them can give me a quarter and I can buy two packs of pixy stix for $1.00." This way we can all enjoy our pixy stix and they would still have money left to buy what they wanted. It was a win/win deal and it worked!

Actually worked a lot better than I had anticipated. After each of my friends received their 3 straws I still had what seemed like tons of pixy stix to get rid of and I couldn't bring them home because I wasn't supposed to be eating candy in the first place. My friends told me not to worry because others my want to some pixy stix once we got to school. I remember as I was running across the schoolyard, I heard a lot of coins jingling in my pocket and when I reached in my pocket, I pulled out a wad of dollar bills along with all of the quarters. I didn't understand how that happened and I was sure I was going to get in big trouble when I got home! So I gave away all the money and forgot about the whole thing.

That memory gave me the idea I needed to pay for my seminars. Even though I was shy and reserved about talking to people, I was going to "sell" candy at school, but on purpose this time! I say "sell" in quotations because I learned how to make sales even though I was too shy to talk to people. To make a long story short, my sister gave me a $20 investment to buy some M&M's, and my new business venture had begun. I was determined, and I was dedicated. I kept reinvesting my profits and ended up with 5 lockers filled with candy and snacks for sale. At one point I was averaging about $200-$300 every day in profits from snacks, candy, and pizza by the slice. I was able to fund my seminar education, help pay for band trips, and even raise money for student government! All because I acted upon my ideas and executed my plans.

If 50% of success is having a winning plan, then the other 50% is actually working the plan. Once you've developed your winning plan, you need to develop a strategy and support system to ensure that you execute your plan. I call this type of winning plan "success insurance". The right plan, properly executed, ensures your success.

Chapter Seven

"O" is for Overcome...
Overcome Your Obstacles

In every adversity, there lies within it the seed of a greater or equivalent benefit
. - Napoleon Hill

In the previous chapter you started developing the beginning of your plan to live life on your own terms. Now that you have done that, grab your pen or pencil. What are your questions, concerns, and fears? How can you overcome them? Where can you find support? Write them all down all down in the space below.

What questions do you have related to your plan? Fears? Concerns?

There are three common reasons why people fail:

- One: They don't select the right goal to begin with and don't get the right support early enough.

- Two: They have the right goal, but they haven't developed a winning plan that ensures their success.

- Three: They have the right goal, have a winning plan that ensures their success, but they are struggling with implementation.

A winning plan is not just any plan. A winning plan is so well thought out and flexible that it almost guarantees your success as long as you execute it. If you struggle with any of the above areas, it's time to invest in a coach. Don't give up until you find the right coach and implement what they coach you to do. Coaching can help you in many areas including the following:

Clarity

Confidence

Consistency

Overwhelm

Fear

Focus

Distractions

Time Management

Saying No

People Pleasing

Delegating

Motivation

BornCEO's don't fail. We either win, or we learn. That doesn't mean we don't face obstacles. One of the greatest ways to overcome obstacles is to surround yourself with others who have overcome and are overcoming them. Some of my favorite examples are people I've had the opportunity to work with over the years. In the following pages you will find a few inspirational examples of other

BornCEO's who didn't let their obstacles stop them from achieving their dreams.

Other BornCEO Stories

Big Tommy Burns, Beast of the Bay Strength

Big Tommy's purpose is to prepare, empower, and equip others to emanate their physical potential into the overall lifestyle of their best health and wellness. In the fitness, personal training, and competitive coaching fields, he physically trains over 25 clients per month and hosts annual competitions and trainings in the sports of Strongman and Powerlifting. The greatest obstacle he faced in building his vision and brand was self-esteem and belief in himself. He struggled to believe that he could provide value to others and package his gift outside the confines of a job structure. He was able to overcome this by challenging himself to push beyond his comfort zone, and he reached out and held on to others' thoughts and beliefs in him until he could believe enough in himself to take the steps he needed to grow his gift and passion. Big Tommy was simply a huge dreamer when he met me, and coming from the arena of sports and football, he understood the power and purpose of how coaching leads to improvement and mastery of practiced skill.

He said, "*For years I would grow in clarity of my vision as I have had consistent conversations with Coach Fard about my BIG vision. We had enough of these conversations and I had taken charge of putting myself in the environments of people who were dreamers and doers. As I watched people take action on their goals and dreams I realized that they were successful not because of all the talent they had, but really because of consistent and persistent effort and pushing beyond the many points of failure. By reaching out to others who had survived and thrived in similar experiences and environments, and receiving tips and pointers for direction of progress, I soon gained the confidence to just take the charge. Coach Fard encouraged me to pursue my vision and reminded me that so many more people needed to see and hear my story and testimony. This is where it all started for me and since then I have been growing a brand and business across Northern California that's grown into six figure income and I'm growing a fitness empire that's helped and empowered many others.*"

Eugene Johnson, CEO of Zryl Co

Eugene's purpose is influence the influencers. His major calling is to help impact the next generation of leaders who will impact the world. A christian minister named Billy Graham who traveled around the world to impact millions of people's lives was asked if he were to do it all over again would he do it the same way and he said if he were to do it all again he would impact the lives of twelve individuals and through them impact the world. Eugene believes that the power to impact the world comes from leaders who know the call on their lives and are willing to walk in that purpose and his calling is to pour into those leaders to help them realize that call and walk it out.

Eugene has been an entrepreneur since he was in junior high school. He says he was an entrepreneur when people thought calling yourself an entrepreneur was an excuse for saying you couldn't find a job. Even though he had worked jobs in the past, his heart has always been in entrepreneurship. Currently he runs a tech startup called ZYRL. ZYRL is a technology company that has simplified operations and marketing for quick service businesses. It starts with the ZYRL Kiosk, a self-service device that allows customers to seamlessly select, customize, and pay for their order all from a gorgeous touchscreen. User data from the ZYRL Kiosk enables businesses to target new and existing customers with automated social media marketing.

One of the greatest obstacles Eugene had to overcome was having one of their potential investors back out last minute. They already started spending money in advance with expectations that the investment was coming through. After the investor pulled out at the last minute, he had seven days to get enough money to save the company and make sure all of their employees got paid. He ended up pulling together hundreds of thousands of dollars in seven days! It was stressful and difficult but exciting to overcome.

In order to overcome, Eugene leveraged relationships with past investors and advisors and he "hit the phones hard". He says, *"I think I might have made over 1000 calls in that 7 days in order to get on the phone with the right people."*

"Working with a someone like Coach Fard will help you find what you have been called to do. He will stretch you to do more and become more. His ability to inspire and motivate all those he coaches is why those who work with him are able to achieve

more than they have ever achieved. He understands the little things that needs to be done in order to win. I remember meeting Coach Fard in a pizza shop in Oklahoma City when I was 18 years old. He immediately pulled out a piece of paper and started drawing out a lesson of success. Ever since I have known him he has been coaching those around him. If you are looking for a coach to take you to the next level I can't imagine finding anyone better than Coach Fard Bell."

Stephen Hill, Minister & Entrepreneur

Stephen's purpose is to empower or help people live life on their own terms. His vehicle is through network marketing. Stephen's greatest obstacle was getting rid of the fear of what people said or thought about his business. He was able to overcome by reading and listening to personal development audios and working with his coach.

He said, *"Working with Coach Fard Bell has allowed me to have confidence in myself. His Coaching and Mentoring and has also helped me strengthen my business and do for others what he has done for me. So, I would say to anyone, we cannot become successful on our own, we need guidance from someone who can see what we cannot, and Coach Bell is just that person."*

J.LeVar Bryan Sr., CEO of The Dad's List

J.LeVar's purpose is helping individuals develop to become the best version of themselves. He is helping them identify and start working in their passions. He is also creating an online community for fathers to share stories and support each other, which he is using to celebrate fatherhood in its many forms. As a Manager for a very successful tech company, he makes a living to support his family, and his daily responsibilities have allowed him to fulfill his passion to some degree. Long term, he is looking to create multiple streams of income, including but not limited to the growth of his online community for fathers. Also, he is looking forward to the long-term success of a company that he plays a major role in. Between those two business ventures and other potentials ideas, his goal is to eventually replace the income of his full time job and pursue his passion full time.

His obstacles have been balancing his professional life with his personal life. J.LeVar has been married since 2007 and he and his wife currently have four children. One of them is autistic and suffers from Sensory Processing Disorder. Maintaining a full time job for a major corporation, and having four kids and two small businesses all at the same time has been the greatest obstacle. He was able to overcome by prayer, learning to be very organized, and by listening to personal development material. He focuses on one project at a time. When he is at work, his mind is at work. When he is investing time and energy in his businesses, that's where his energy is. When he is with family, they get his full attention.

"I met Coach Fard Bell in 2003 and he led an organization that first introduced me to the concept of working harder on myself than I do on my business! I love his ability to see beyond the obvious, regardless of who he's talking to, so he can provide real solutions. When talking to him, ideas seem to click more and inspiration immediately follows afterwards. I find Coach Fard to be an extremely resourceful individual and he genuinely has a desire to see others succeed. His mentoring eliminates excuses and requires activity from the mentee."

Joy Olivier, Small Business Consultant

Joy's purpose is to help business owners maximize the power of relationship networking to grow their businesses. Oftentimes business owners focus on the day-to-day operations and miss the amazing resources all around them that can be helpful to building their business. Teaching business owners to identify those opportunities IS her dream. Before coaching, she said she had no idea that she could work in her passion. She focused on an industry she had grown up with, which was the insurance industry. Although she became super successful in insurance, it wasn't her passion. However, she says if it wasn't for her insurance career she would not have been able to work her passion. Joy started with one client and now serves over 6000 families. Her greatest obstacle was that she thinking her passion was just a dream. She thought it was something that was unattainable and just a place where her mind could wander. She overcame her obstacle through coaching which helped her realize that she could actually live her dream if she put better systems in place, gave herself goals to achieve, and had a purpose for everything she did. Joy said she became more structured, hired a bigger sales team to support her insurance business, found the courage to "network up". She found and met with people who did business better than she did.

"Coach Fard Bell, was really able to identify the areas where I needed extra support. He helped me come up with my attainable vision and gave me the confidence to take a couple major leaps of faith. He has incredible knowledge that can be applied in all industries which is beneficial when coaching business leaders. He has a gentle nature and an encouraging spirit about him which makes him easy to work with. It wasn't long until I had the confidence in myself and those around me to make my passions come true."

Michael Loubier Founder/CEO Loubier Gourmet

Michael's purpose right now is to build multinational million dollar businesses to fund the Kingdom of God. BBQ Sauce is one vehicle. This year's goal is to make his products available in 1250 retail stores and through 200 food service clients. He said the hardest obstacle is being a dad, husband, and business owner a the same time. Losing his mom, dad, uncle, cousin, 2 dogs, a close friend in the last 3 - 4 years has taken a toll. But, he says that doing business is the easy part when you are aligned correctly and God is #1. Michael overcame by putting God first in everything he does and realizing that at the end of the day, money is just a vehicle and a tool do His work.

"God has used Coach Fard as a tool and that is the most important thing. It was a phone conversation with him, that led me to my relationship with Christ. I think if we all don't worry about who gets the credit and we don't compare ourselves with everyone else, we all can do so much more for God's kingdom. Besides I've never seen a U-Haul truck behind a hearse at a funeral."

Peter Quiales, Direct Sales & Dadpreneur

Peter's dream is to live a lifestyle on his own terms where he can wake up in the morning without an alarm clock because living out his passion for life is what gets him up. His dream is to be a successful Dadpreneur where he is a successful and involved father as well as a successful entrepreneur. He sees himself becoming an international public speaker who inspires millions of people to take accountability and change and improve their lives. He plans on having non-profit organizations that help teach people of all ages life, social, and economic skills to improve their own lives. Peter comes from poverty so he feels it's important to have and teach skills that were never taught to millions of others in poverty. He is fulfilling his dreams and purpose in the direct sales and network marketing industry. He chose it because he recently obtained his bachelor's degree in business with a concentration in finance. Peter almost went the corporate America route in business but he didn't want to be a part of a for-profit and bottom line oriented business model. The biggest obstacle Peter had to overcome was to finish college while having two small children. He overcame his obstacles by reading books on leadership and self-help, as well as reading motivational books and watching videos that helped him learn new skills about accountability, self-discipline, responsibility, vision, work ethic, integrity, and time management, etc. He said they all helped him internally and externally be a better person. He sought mentors, and he now realizes that he is a lifelong learner because he wants to continue growing in life.

"I want to mention the importance and value of mentors both living and dead. What I mean by that is that I have read numerous books by the same authors that I feel have taught me so much that I feel like they were my mentors in a sense. The same for videos and podcasts that I have listened to. And living mentors. I have a few mentors now that help me. I have one mentor in particular who is an actual certified life coach who does it for a living. I feel like the universe worked itself out when we met and crossed paths in life. His name is Coach Fard Bell. He has helped me by reassuring me about everything I've been learning over the years. Coach Fard Bell was able to help me improve what I was already doing right and was able to help me understand why and what I was doing wrong that wasn't giving me what I wanted in life. Mindset is so important and understanding why we think the way we think is so important. When I think of Coach Bell, I think, "Effective, Compassionate, and

Empowering". Being able to work with someone who can know and see your inconsistencies and not hold it against you but instead try to get you to realize and overcome them is so important and that's exactly what my mentors did for me. I do feel that Coach Fard and my other mentors have improved my life for the better. Why learn through trial and error when you can learn through experience and leverage."

Hannah Bell, Mompreneur & Founder/CEO Mommy & Me Stockton

Hannah was never was connected to her purpose. Like me, she felt like she had all the pieces of a jigsaw puzzle without seeing the cover of the box. She knew she loved children, singing, and performing. She also knew she had a heart for bringing people together and helping them feel safe and welcome. It wasn't until being mentored by Coach Fard Bell that she really connected with her vision and started on the path to where she is today. Even though her Master's Degree was in something completely different, she knew in her heart that she was called to work with babies and young children, she just didn't know how.

Everything started coming together when Hannah was searching for activities to do with her then two year old son when she realized he needed more social activities to participate in. The mommy & me activities in her local area were slim to none, so she started her own music class, and then it grew from there! Her company, Mommy and Me Stockton, with its menu of fun activities and events for babies, toddlers, and preschoolers, took off like a rocket ship within its first six months. Their activities became so popular and in such high demand that new locations were being planned within the first year, and more talks of expansion were being considered beyond that.

Hannah's biggest obstacle has been trusting the process of becoming an entrepreneur. She explains, *"This includes a lot of faith, strong work ethic, and definitely letting go of my fear of rejection. I've overcome these obstacles by focusing more on the promise than on the journey, and by sharing my vision with all who are interested, and then asking for help from those that have bought into my vision too."*

"Being coached/mentored is critical in navigating the rough waters of entrepreneurship, especially for a formally trained educator like myself. Entrepreneurs live by a whole different set of core values that need to be learned. I am so grateful for the years of coaching that I received by Coach Fard Bell and I know I wouldn't be where I am if it weren't for him."

Steve Bacon, High Performance Coach

Steve's purpose is to help people breakthrough limiting beliefs. His passion is coaching and empowering high performers to achieve goals that thought were impossible to achieve. His greatest obstacle was overcoming self-doubt and limiting beliefs about himself. He overcame his obstacle by investing in high level personal development and coaching.

"Coach Fard has a natural gift for asking surgical like questions to get to the root cause of a problem. Working with him gave me the confidence that I was more than capable of becoming a successful entrepreneur and coach."

Angela Benjamin, Mompreneur & Real Estate Investor

Angela's purpose is currently being fulfilled. She is a full-time mom and entrepreneur. She said she inspires her children and other youth to reach for their dreams no matter how far away they seem. She is using real estate as a vehicle to make a living and she teaches to make a difference. The greatest obstacle she overcame was believing that she could get started when she didn't really have any money. She overcame it by attending a lot of networking events where she met others who had success, and also by studying and by taking action.

"Coaching with Coach Fard Bell has given me a place to feel comfortable about sharing my real business challenges. I leave each session empowered with the tools to solve problems and take right actions. I am amazed at how Coach Fard detangles entrepreneurial knots and how he shrinks what looks like a major mountain, to a tiny pebble."

Sharon Twitty, Professional Model & Actress

Sharon said, "*Since age 12 when I gave my 1st speech at the Cherry Blossom Festival in DC in front of my whole school class and former Mayor Marion Barry, I felt my love for being in character and in front of a crowd. It was then that I realized I loved to perform. Ironically, in my late teens I was prophesied to in church that I was going to be a model. Today, my purpose and passion is a reality. I am a professional model and actress. I am a performer. During high school I performed after classes in local youth groups. I attended a modeling school and then worked full-time while part time getting experience modeling and acting whenever I could. Basically, I started off working full-time on my living and part time on my passion. I also joined a network marketing company and gained entrepreneurial skills and mindset in the process. This is how I met Coach Bell. My greatest obstacle to get where I am was absolutely quitting my job and being self-employed. My special talents and purpose that were revealed to me as a little teen required a harder path in life. To succeed as an entertainer you will not be living the typical employee 9 to 5 routine. You have to travel often for auditions and work. Your manager and/or agent needs you to be available when they book you for their clients. The higher you go in the industry you have to have a flexible schedule. Because of this my full-time job became a major obstacle. I had to make a decision. I already invested years of time, energy and money into my purpose. My purpose is ready to make room for me now that I've planted all the seeds. Now it was time to have faith that if I am called to do something then I am called to do it 100%. I made the decision. I planned my exit and I quit my good job for my greater calling."*

"Thanks to the skills I learned in Network Marketing I was molded to work hard and understood the reality of doing the opposite of the masses to become successful. In less than two years, I accomplished more than double in the modeling/acting industry now that I overcame my obstacle and have a flexible schedule then in the previous five years not doing what I knew I needed to do. More than a financial decision it was a mental decision. I overcame my obstacle by making a mental decision. A mental decision to do what it takes."

She said, *"There are people along my journey who I have to thank for my success. The greatest of those is Coach Fard. I met him when I was exiting my teens. I was excited about life and learning the ropes in entertainment. He seemed even more excited about life and coaching his team of business associates. This drew me to him. His undying love to help others break free of the chains of mediocrity and become great living the life they wanted to live and with financial freedom. I wanted and was working on being great too! His enthusiasm and passion made me want to learn what he knew. I knew I could use the life and business nuggets that he aggressively pursued. It is because of my business mentoring from Coach Bell that I gained financial wisdom, entrepreneurial habits and mindsets, massive people skills and how to handle all levels of rejection. All of which I used in my journey to become a professional model and actress. Without Coach Bell's one on one and group mentorship over the years I will not be as prepared as I am today. God put him in my life for a reason. I am forever thankful."*

Helen Molina, Real Estate Professional

Helen said, *"When I started with Coach Fard I was very insecure of myself. I lacked confidence and had a lot fear of going into an uncomfortable place in my career as a Real Estate professional. He walked me through the process of believing in my abilities and allowed me to see myself the way God saw me. In only 13 weeks he made a huge difference in my career life. I feel comfortable with who I am and most importantly I have learned to love what I do because all the insecurities and doubts are no longer there. Thank you Coach Fard!"*

Michael Bailey, Small Business Owner

Michael said, "My passion and purpose is to be an advocate for autistic and sexually abused children. My plan was to build a significant passive income outside of my job."

Michael's greatest obstacle was working full time as a leader in a government agency while running a locksmith company, as well as being active in church and at the same time, being available for his mother who was suffering from dementia before she passed.

"Coach Fard Bell played a huge role in teaching me how to build my business while handling all of my priorities with only slivers of time for contacting, inviting, and presentations. But I would say the biggest impact and awakening I received from Coach Bell's mentoring was discovering what I was truly passionate about (from the heart) which was becoming an advocate for autistic and sexually abused children. After a powerful conversation with Coach I became clear on the path to pursue my purpose. Because I was building passive income I was able to retire early from the government in Dec 2016 and be with mom until she passed away in April 2017. For that I will forever be grateful."

LaTisha Randolph, Home-Based Business Mompreneur

LaTisha said, *"For over a decade, I worked my home-based business spare time while maintaining a full-time job. At some point, my plan was to walk away from my job and live life on my own terms. After my husband and I had our third kid, my dream of becoming a stay-at-home mom became even more desirable. Even though I wanted to be with the kids, I still wished to contribute financially to the family without sacrificing my professional identity. We decided that I would leave my corporate job and only work my network marketing business. I was afraid. I had to overcome the fear of failure and of the unknown. I also had to learn how to navigate business without the structure and discipline that a traditional job offers.*

"Coach Bell provided me with a step-by-step plan that led me in the direction of success. He explained what to expect, how to start and how to maintain my business. His guidance over the last 5 years not only helped me step out of my comfort zone but also

helped me multiply my income many times over resulting in a 700% overall increase! This gentleman literally helped me breakthrough layers of mental and emotional barriers that were limiting my progress. He freed me from the chains I put on myself. Now, I successfully work from home whenever I choose while taking care of my family. I continue on the path of improvement and higher levels of success. With the skills Coach Bell has taught me, I am confident that I will achieve my vision within record time. I am eternally grateful for his coaching and am certain that I could not have done any of this without him."

Now it's your turn. Fill in the following answers..m

YOUR NAME:

- What's Your Dream/Purpose:

- What's Your Plan:

- Greatest Obstacles You Are Facing:

- How You Can Overcome:

Conclusion

You have now discovered the 7 steps to claiming your freedom & living your purpose. You have awakened the BornCEO within you. Remember, the process doesn't end here. This is just the beginning. Now it's time to get started. You have everything inside of you to become who you were born to be and do what you were born to do. Everything else you need will be provided for you as you embrace your journey.

Remember that you are not alone. You have an entire support community backing you within the BornCEO family.

Declarations

Repeat after me:

"There's a problem I was born to solve!"

"I am already gifted to solve the problem I was born to solve!"

"All the money I'll ever need is hiding behind my purpose!"

"I am the BornCEO of my mind!"

"I am the BornCEO of my time!"

"I am the BornCEO of my choices!"

"I was born to rule my domain!"

"I. Was. Born. To. Rule!"

"BECOME WHO YOU WERE BORN TO BE"
By Coach Fard Bell

"There's somewhere a King who owns the Earth, and everything in it at large.

He built it from scratch and set it all up, but placed His kids in charge.

He gave them a gift to learn to use and told them to heed His voice.

Use it wisely and win, Use it poorly and lose This great gift, is the gift of choice.

Remember that you can choose to win. And that you can choose to be free...

Because it's never too late for you to become the leader you were born to be!"

Additional Resources

"We're all BornCEO's... We just need the right coaching."

You are not alone.

Get the support you deserve. Here are your resources:

Create your free account at www.BornCEO.com

(After you create your free account, login and go into the "BornCEO Academy Welcome Center" to follow the 3 steps to accelerating your growth).

Let Us Know How We Can Best Support You.

www.CoachFardBell.com/support

Life & Business Resources

To get your take the Best Year Ever Workshop Online and download your workbook:
www.CoachFardBell.com/bye

Join BornCEO Academy achieve your life and business goals faster:
www.CoachFardBell.com/club

Direct Sales & Network Marketing Support

Generic Network Marketing Online Bootcamp: www.CoachFardBell.com/bootcamp

To join my generic Network Marketing Coaching Mastermind to multiply your income in Network Marketing: www.CoachFardBell.com/mlm

To subscribe to our free newsletter, join our free online community, connect with the Born CEO Coaching team, or to book Coach Fard Bell to speak at your event: www.BornCEO.com

Remember who you are…

You are the BornCEO of You, Inc.
You were Born to Rule!